That's the One!

Copyright © QEB Publishing, Inc. 2007

First published in the United States by
QEB Publishing, Inc.
Wrigley, Suite A
Irvine CA 92618

www.qeb-publishing.com

Library of Congress Control Number: 2006038443

ISBN 978 1 84538 671 9

Written by Bernard Ashley
Edited by Clare Weaver
Designed by Alix Wood
Illustrated by Janee Trasler
Consultancy by Anne Faundez

Printed in China

That's the One!

Bernard Ashley

Illustrated by Janee Trasler

QEB Publishing

It was Friday and Billy's mom and dad had an invitation to a party. But the invitation had been stuck in the mail, and the party was the next night. So soon!

"I want something different to wear," said Billy's mom. "A new look!"
"Sorry, but I can't help you choose," Billy's dad said.
"I've got to go to work."
Billy's eyes lit up.

I'll come! I'll help you choose—and I can spend my birthday money from Nana.

Good idea!

said Dad.

Billy's dad was a fitter at **Fast-Fix.**

Billy liked to sit in the office and watch his dad at work. But today, Billy had a job to do as well.

Mom drove them into town. Try It On was the best place to look for Mom's new clothes. "Something different!" she said.

Try It On

OPEN

Jack and Jill's

First, Mom chose a pretty blouse and a leather skirt with tassels. She showed them to the shop assistant, went into the changing rooms—and out came a cowgirl, like in a western movie!

"That's the one!" said Billy.
And it gave him an idea.
He could choose a cowboy
hat as his birthday present.

"I look like I've lost my horse," Mom said, shaking her head.

Next, she picked a short dress with black-and-white stripes.

She showed it to the shop assistant, went into the changing rooms—and out came a sporty girl soccer player, like on the women's team at the park.

CUP FINAL

"That's the one!" said Billy.
And it gave him a different idea.
He could choose a soccer ball for himself.

But Mom shook her head.
"That's not a winner!"

Then, she chose a long, bright dress with patterns of exotic flowers. She showed it to the shop assistant, went into the changing rooms—and out came a girl from Jamaica.

"That's the one!" said Billy.
And it gave him another idea.

He could choose a steel drum as his present.

"It doesn't bang the drum for me," Mom said. Now she chose a white, silk blouse and matching scarf.

She showed them to the shop assistant, in she went—and out came a pirate, as exciting as Captain Annie in Billy's *Sea Fighters* book.

"That's the one!" said Billy. And what about a pirate's telescope for himself?

"Doesn't grab me," Mom said.
Her final choice was a pretty, green top
with a wide, white collar and matching pants.
She showed them to the shop assistant,
in she went for the last time—and out
came Robin Hood.

"That's the one!" said Billy.
Great—a bow and arrow as his present!

"Misses the target with me,"
Mom sighed.
So, they went to Jack and Jill's
to choose Billy's present.

Hats 2 go

Mom was
disappointed that
she hadn't found
anything to wear, but
Billy looked high and
low until he saw just
the thing—

a little, red sports car.

Dad came in wearing his dirty overalls.

How did you do?   Dad asked.

But suddenly,
Mom was giving Dad
a long, hard look.

Wait and see!

Billy frowned.
He didn't get it.
Not at all.

It was the party night and Dad was waiting to go.

Are you ready yet?
We're going to be late! he called up the stairs.

"Almost ready!"
Mom shouted back.

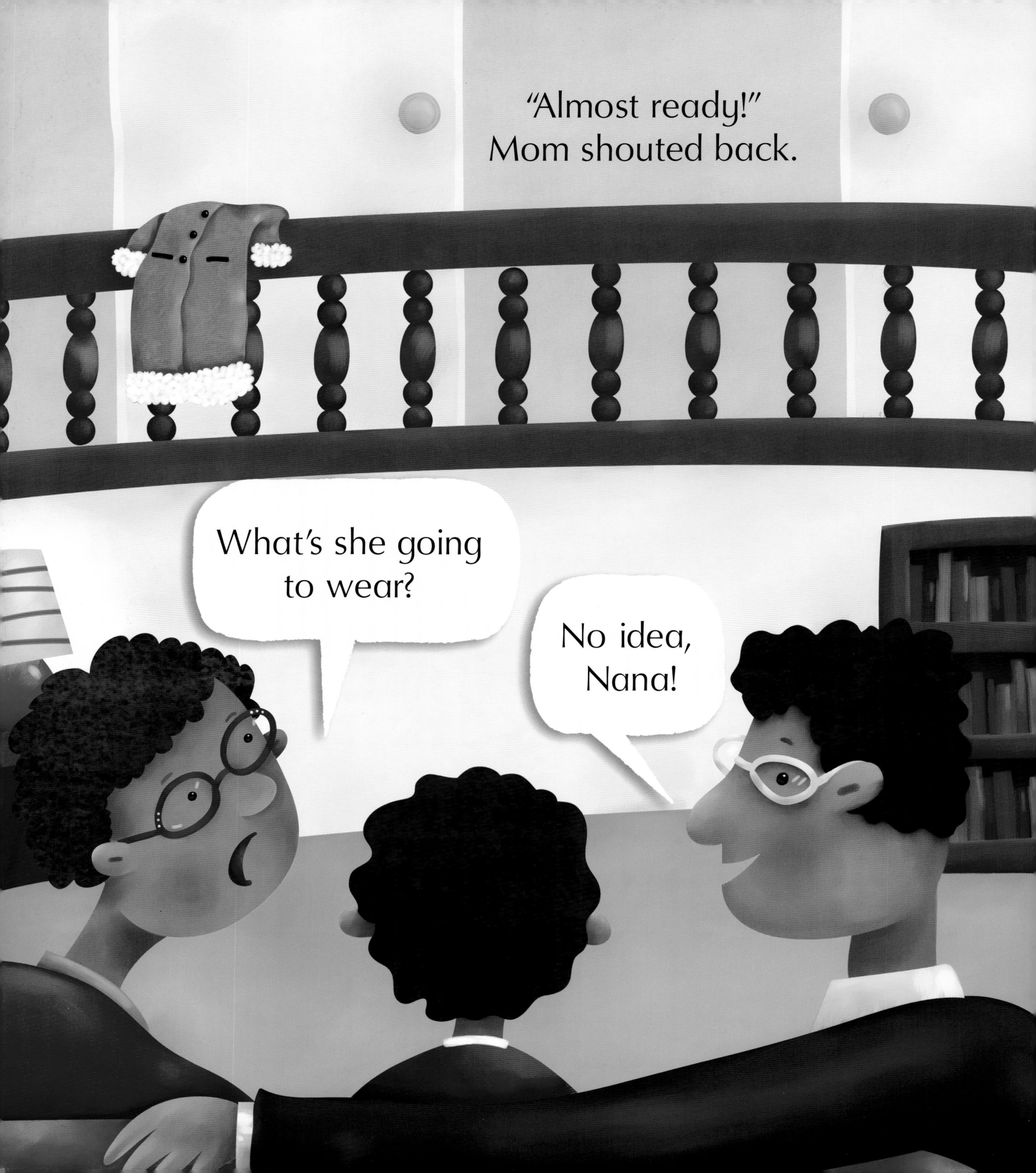

They heard the bedroom door open. Mom was coming! And she looked lovely.

Her necklace and her earrings sparkled and so did her shiny, red shoes.

She couldn't have chosen anything more beautiful to wear than Dad's clean dungarees.

"That's the one!" said Billy and Dad together.

Notes for Teachers and Parents

- *That's the One!* is a realistic story that connects to Billy's fantasies. Talking and laughing about the pictures and the text helps involve the children in the book and develops reading and thinking skills.

- The story line offers opportunities to share stories of cowboys and pirates with the children. Do the children know what job cowboys and cowgirls used to do? "Captain Annie" is a made-up pirate name. Have the children read any pirate stories or seen any pirate films? What were some of the pirates' names? Which plays or performances have the children seen? Which characters were in them?

- Billy's daydreams about soccer can lead to a discussion about the sport. What are the names of the children's favorite soccer players? Do any of the children play soccer? Have any of the children been to watch a soccer game?

- Have any of the children ever taken part in a carnival or fancy-dress parade? What did they wear? Look out for news coverage of Caribbean carnivals as well as stories and books from and about the West Indies to show the children.

- Provide a dress-up box for imaginative play. The children can act out the different characters in the story—for example; a mechanic at *Fast-Fix*, a soccer player, or the clothing store assistant.

- Play can lead to stories. Note down the children's stories, then write them on good paper (or print them from the computer) to make a special book for sharing. The children could illustrate the stories with their own drawings.

- Children are surrounded by words, at home and in the street, and they can be useful in reading. How many of the words around them can the children read? Can they decode any words phonetically? Remember to keep everything light and fun, and stop when the children get bored or frustrated.

- The illustrations might inspire the children to think of new stories. For example, why is the woman in the background trying on hats? Can the children make up a story about her? When Billy is driving on the open road, where is he going—and where would the children like to go? Encourage the children to imagine what adventures could be had on the way.